DAILY KNITTING AGENDA

Date:

TO DO:

KNITTING PRIORITIES:

KNITTING QUOTE OF THE DAY:

KNITTING TAKS OF THE DAY

NOTES

DAILY KNITTING AGENDA

Date:

TO DO:

- [ ]
- [ ]
- [ ]
- [ ]
- [ ]
- [ ]

KNITTING PRIORITIES:

KNITTING QUOTE OF THE DAY:

KNITTING TAKS OF THE DAY

NOTES

DAILY KNITTING AGENDA

Date: _____

TO DO:

KNITTING PRIORITIES:

KNITTING QUOTE OF THE DAY:

KNITTING TAKS OF THE DAY

NOTES

DAILY KNITTING AGENDA

Date:

TO DO:

KNITTING PRIORITIES:

KNITTING QUOTE OF THE DAY:

KNITTING TAKS OF THE DAY

NOTES

DAILY KNITTING AGENDA

Date: _____

TO DO:

KNITTING PRIORITIES:

KNITTING QUOTE OF THE DAY:

KNITTING TAKS OF THE DAY

NOTES

DAILY KNITTING AGENDA

Date: _____

TO DO:
- ☐ _____
- ☐ _____
- ☐ _____
- ☐ _____
- ☐ _____
- ☐ _____
- ☐ _____

KNITTING PRIORITIES:

KNITTING QUOTE OF THE DAY:

KNITTING TAKS OF THE DAY

NOTES

DAILY KNITTING AGENDA

Date:

TO DO:

KNITTING PRIORITIES:

KNITTING QUOTE OF THE DAY:

KNITTING TAKS OF THE DAY

NOTES

DAILY KNITTING AGENDA

Date:

TO DO:

- _____
- _____
- _____
- _____
- _____
- _____
- _____

KNITTING PRIORITIES:

KNITTING QUOTE OF THE DAY:

KNITTING TAKS OF THE DAY

NOTES

DAILY KNITTING AGENDA

Date:

TO DO:

KNITTING PRIORITIES:

KNITTING QUOTE OF THE DAY:

KNITTING TAKS OF THE DAY

NOTES

DAILY KNITTING AGENDA

Date: _____

TO DO:

☐ _____
☐ _____
☐ _____
☐ _____
☐ _____
☐ _____
☐ _____

KNITTING PRIORITIES:

KNITTING QUOTE OF THE DAY:

KNITTING TAKS OF THE DAY

NOTES

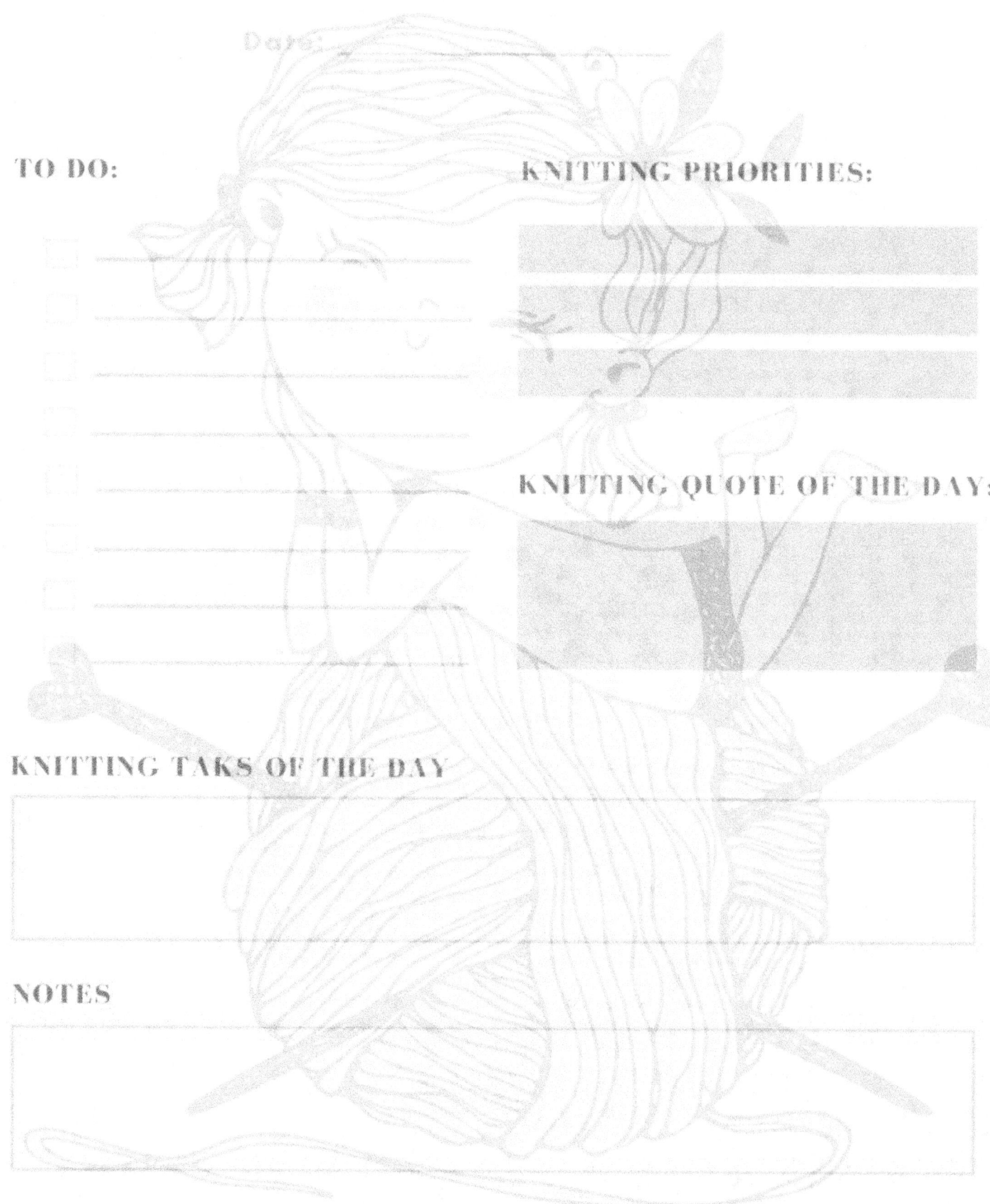

DAILY KNITTING AGENDA

Date:

TO DO:

KNITTING PRIORITIES:

KNITTING QUOTE OF THE DAY:

KNITTING TAKS OF THE DAY

NOTES

DAILY KNITTING AGENDA

Date:

TO DO:

KNITTING PRIORITIES:

KNITTING QUOTE OF THE DAY:

KNITTING TAKS OF THE DAY

NOTES

DAILY KNITTING AGENDA

Date:

TO DO:

KNITTING PRIORITIES:

KNITTING QUOTE OF THE DAY:

KNITTING TAKS OF THE DAY

NOTES

DAILY KNITTING AGENDA

Date: _____

TO DO:

- ☐ _____
- ☐ _____
- ☐ _____
- ☐ _____
- ☐ _____
- ☐ _____
- ☐ _____

KNITTING PRIORITIES:

KNITTING QUOTE OF THE DAY:

KNITTING TAKS OF THE DAY

NOTES

DAILY KNITTING AGENDA

Date:

TO DO:

KNITTING PRIORITIES:

KNITTING QUOTE OF THE DAY:

KNITTING TAKS OF THE DAY

NOTES

DAILY KNITTING AGENDA

Date:

TO DO:

KNITTING PRIORITIES:

KNITTING QUOTE OF THE DAY:

KNITTING TAKS OF THE DAY

NOTES

DAILY KNITTING AGENDA

Date:

TO DO:

KNITTING PRIORITIES:

KNITTING QUOTE OF THE DAY:

KNITTING TAKS OF THE DAY

NOTES

DAILY KNITTING AGENDA

Date: _____

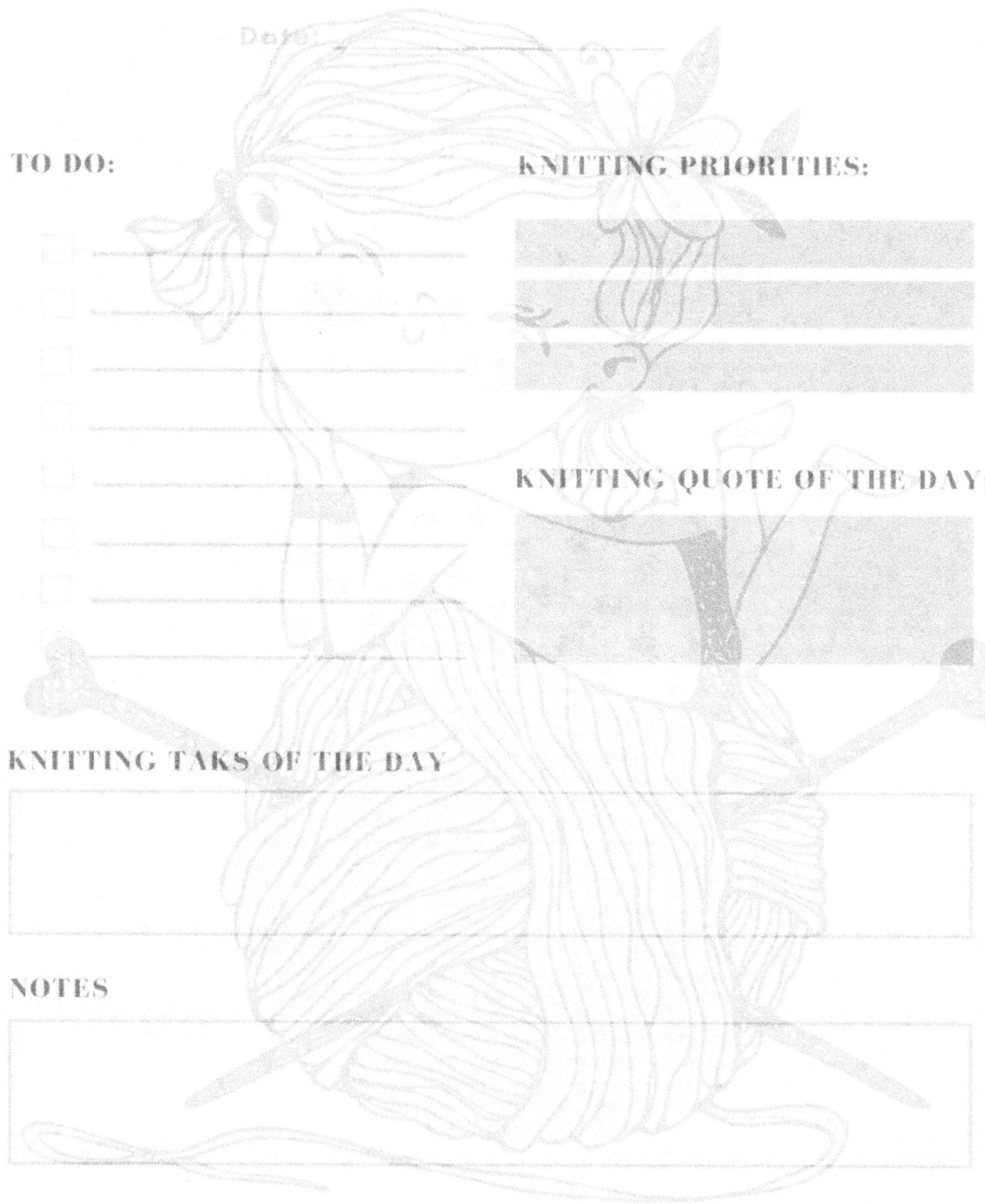

TO DO:
- [ ] _____
- [ ] _____
- [ ] _____
- [ ] _____
- [ ] _____
- [ ] _____

KNITTING PRIORITIES:

KNITTING QUOTE OF THE DAY:

KNITTING TAKS OF THE DAY

NOTES

DAILY KNITTING AGENDA

Date: _____

TO DO:

KNITTING PRIORITIES:

KNITTING QUOTE OF THE DAY:

KNITTING TAKS OF THE DAY

NOTES

DAILY KNITTING AGENDA

Date:

TO DO:

-
-
-
-
-
-
-

KNITTING PRIORITIES:

KNITTING QUOTE OF THE DAY:

KNITTING TAKS OF THE DAY

NOTES

DAILY KNITTING AGENDA

Date:

TO DO:

KNITTING PRIORITIES:

KNITTING QUOTE OF THE DAY:

KNITTING TAKS OF THE DAY

NOTES

DAILY KNITTING AGENDA

Date:

TO DO:

-
-
-
-
-
-
-

KNITTING PRIORITIES:

KNITTING QUOTE OF THE DAY:

KNITTING TAKS OF THE DAY

NOTES

DAILY KNITTING AGENDA

Date:

TO DO:

KNITTING PRIORITIES:

KNITTING QUOTE OF THE DAY:

KNITTING TAKS OF THE DAY

NOTES

DAILY KNITTING AGENDA

Date:

TO DO:

KNITTING PRIORITIES:

KNITTING QUOTE OF THE DAY:

KNITTING TAKS OF THE DAY

NOTES

DAILY KNITTING AGENDA

Date:

TO DO:

KNITTING PRIORITIES:

KNITTING QUOTE OF THE DAY:

KNITTING TAKS OF THE DAY

NOTES

DAILY KNITTING AGENDA

Date:

TO DO:

- [ ]
- [ ]
- [ ]
- [ ]
- [ ]
- [ ]
- [ ]

KNITTING PRIORITIES:

KNITTING QUOTE OF THE DAY:

KNITTING TAKS OF THE DAY

NOTES

DAILY KNITTING AGENDA

Date:

TO DO:

KNITTING PRIORITIES:

KNITTING QUOTE OF THE DAY:

KNITTING TAKS OF THE DAY

NOTES

DAILY KNITTING AGENDA

Date:

TO DO:

KNITTING PRIORITIES:

KNITTING QUOTE OF THE DAY:

KNITTING TAKS OF THE DAY

NOTES

DAILY KNITTING AGENDA

Date:

TO DO:

KNITTING PRIORITIES:

KNITTING QUOTE OF THE DAY:

KNITTING TAKS OF THE DAY

NOTES

DAILY KNITTING AGENDA

Date: _____

TO DO:

- ☐ _____
- ☐ _____
- ☐ _____
- ☐ _____
- ☐ _____
- ☐ _____
- ☐ _____

KNITTING PRIORITIES:

KNITTING QUOTE OF THE DAY:

KNITTING TAKS OF THE DAY

NOTES

DAILY KNITTING AGENDA

Date: _____

TO DO:

KNITTING PRIORITIES:

KNITTING QUOTE OF THE DAY:

KNITTING TAKS OF THE DAY

NOTES

DAILY KNITTING AGENDA

Date:

TO DO:

KNITTING PRIORITIES:

KNITTING QUOTE OF THE DAY:

KNITTING TAKS OF THE DAY

NOTES

DAILY KNITTING AGENDA

Date:

TO DO:

KNITTING PRIORITIES:

KNITTING QUOTE OF THE DAY:

KNITTING TAKS OF THE DAY

NOTES

DAILY KNITTING AGENDA

Date:

TO DO:

-
-
-
-
-
-
-

KNITTING PRIORITIES:

KNITTING QUOTE OF THE DAY:

KNITTING TAKS OF THE DAY

NOTES

DAILY KNITTING AGENDA

Date: _____

TO DO:

KNITTING PRIORITIES:

KNITTING QUOTE OF THE DAY:

KNITTING TAKS OF THE DAY

NOTES

DAILY KNITTING AGENDA

Date:

TO DO:

KNITTING PRIORITIES:

KNITTING QUOTE OF THE DAY:

KNITTING TAKS OF THE DAY

NOTES

DAILY KNITTING AGENDA

Date:

TO DO:

KNITTING PRIORITIES:

KNITTING QUOTE OF THE DAY:

KNITTING TAKS OF THE DAY

NOTES

DAILY KNITTING AGENDA

Date:

TO DO:

- [ ]
- [ ]
- [ ]
- [ ]
- [ ]
- [ ]
- [ ]
- [ ]

KNITTING PRIORITIES:

KNITTING QUOTE OF THE DAY:

KNITTING TAKS OF THE DAY

NOTES

DAILY KNITTING AGENDA

Date:

TO DO:

KNITTING PRIORITIES:

KNITTING QUOTE OF THE DAY:

KNITTING TAKS OF THE DAY

NOTES

DAILY KNITTING AGENDA

Date:

TO DO:

KNITTING PRIORITIES:

KNITTING QUOTE OF THE DAY:

KNITTING TAKS OF THE DAY

NOTES

DAILY KNITTING AGENDA

Date:

TO DO:

KNITTING PRIORITIES:

KNITTING QUOTE OF THE DAY:

KNITTING TAKS OF THE DAY

NOTES

DAILY KNITTING AGENDA

Date:

TO DO:

KNITTING PRIORITIES:

KNITTING QUOTE OF THE DAY:

KNITTING TAKS OF THE DAY

NOTES

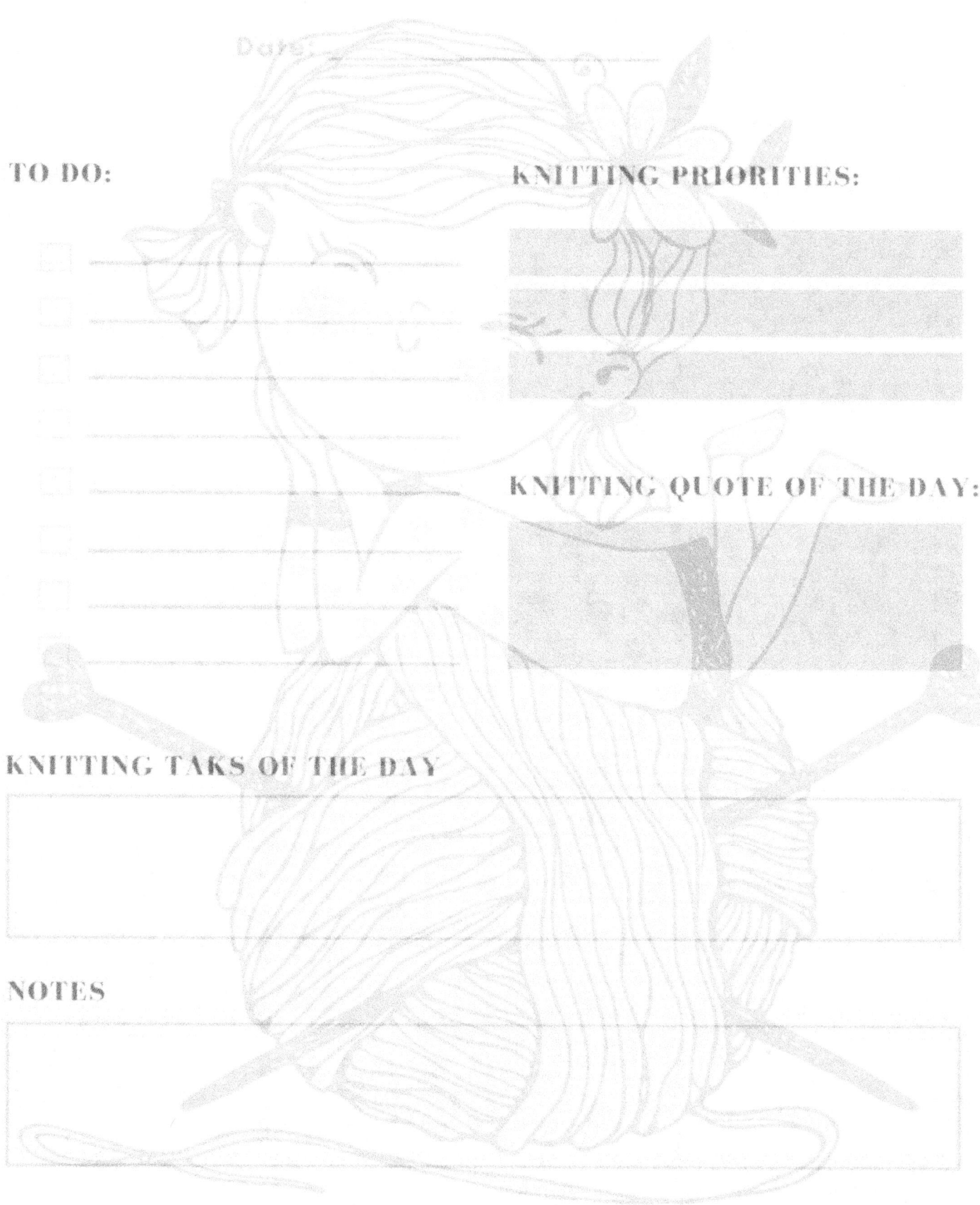

DAILY KNITTING AGENDA

Date: _____

TO DO:

KNITTING PRIORITIES:

KNITTING QUOTE OF THE DAY:

KNITTING TAKS OF THE DAY

NOTES

DAILY KNITTING AGENDA

Date:

TO DO:

KNITTING PRIORITIES:

KNITTING QUOTE OF THE DAY:

KNITTING TAKS OF THE DAY

NOTES

DAILY KNITTING AGENDA

Date:

TO DO:

KNITTING PRIORITIES:

KNITTING QUOTE OF THE DAY:

KNITTING TAKS OF THE DAY

NOTES

DAILY KNITTING AGENDA

Date: _____

TO DO:
- ☐ _____
- ☐ _____
- ☐ _____
- ☐ _____
- ☐ _____
- ☐ _____
- ☐ _____
- ☐ _____

KNITTING PRIORITIES:

KNITTING QUOTE OF THE DAY:

KNITTING TAKS OF THE DAY

NOTES

DAILY KNITTING AGENDA

Date:

TO DO:

KNITTING PRIORITIES:

KNITTING QUOTE OF THE DAY:

KNITTING TAKS OF THE DAY

NOTES

DAILY KNITTING AGENDA

Date:

TO DO:

-
-
-
-
-
-
-
-

KNITTING PRIORITIES:

KNITTING QUOTE OF THE DAY:

KNITTING TAKS OF THE DAY

NOTES

DAILY KNITTING AGENDA

Date:

TO DO:

KNITTING PRIORITIES:

KNITTING QUOTE OF THE DAY:

KNITTING TAKS OF THE DAY

NOTES

DAILY KNITTING AGENDA

Date:

TO DO:

-
-
-
-
-
-

KNITTING PRIORITIES:

KNITTING QUOTE OF THE DAY:

KNITTING TAKS OF THE DAY

NOTES

DAILY KNITTING AGENDA

Date: _____

TO DO:

KNITTING PRIORITIES:

KNITTING QUOTE OF THE DAY:

KNITTING TAKS OF THE DAY

NOTES

DAILY KNITTING AGENDA

Date:

TO DO:

KNITTING PRIORITIES:

KNITTING QUOTE OF THE DAY:

KNITTING TAKS OF THE DAY

NOTES

DAILY KNITTING AGENDA

Date:

TO DO:

KNITTING PRIORITIES:

KNITTING QUOTE OF THE DAY:

KNITTING TAKS OF THE DAY

NOTES

DAILY KNITTING AGENDA

Date:

TO DO:

- [ ] _____
- [ ] _____
- [ ] _____
- [ ] _____
- [ ] _____
- [ ] _____
- [ ] _____

KNITTING PRIORITIES:

KNITTING QUOTE OF THE DAY:

KNITTING TAKS OF THE DAY

NOTES

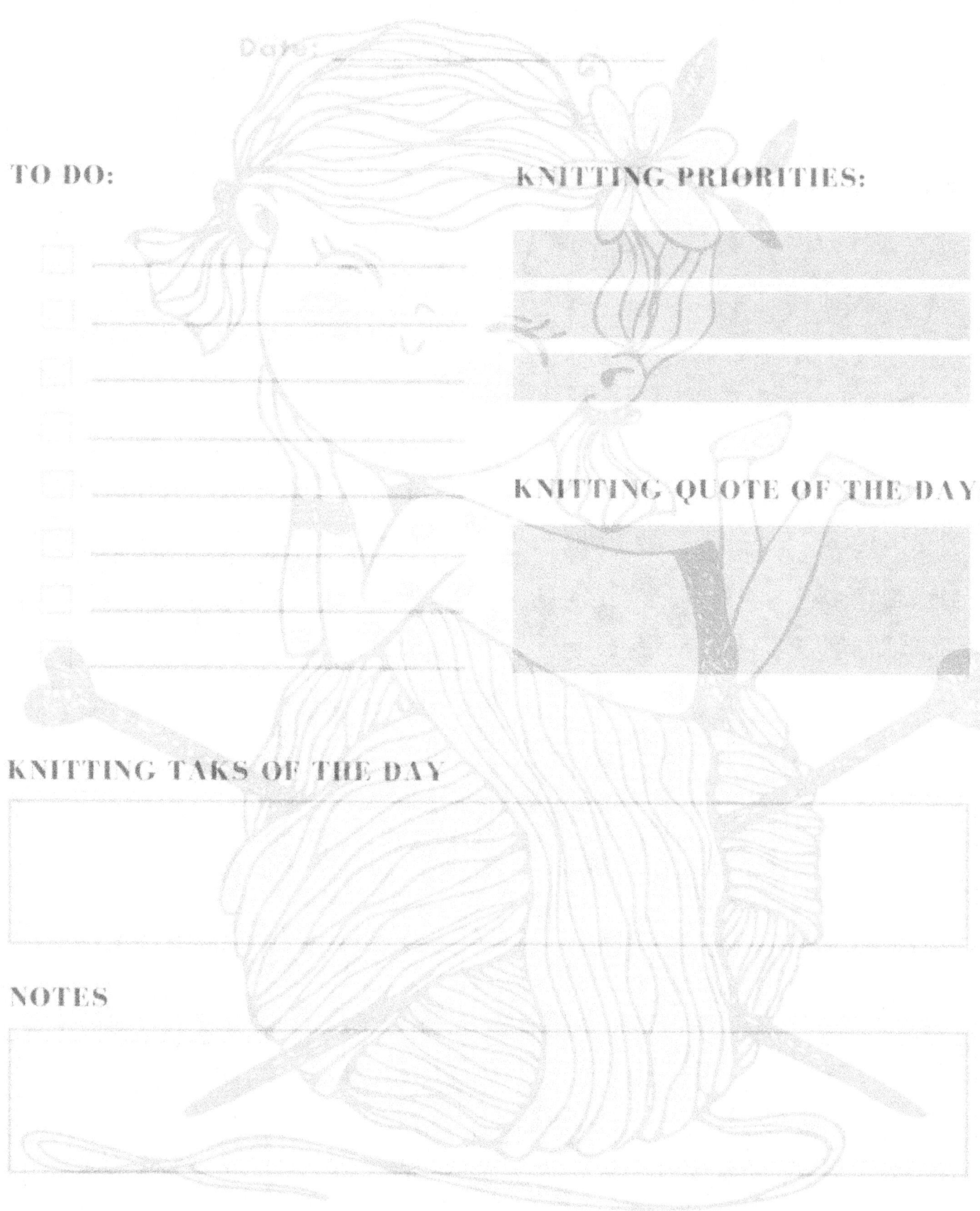

DAILY KNITTING AGENDA

Date:

TO DO:

KNITTING PRIORITIES:

KNITTING QUOTE OF THE DAY:

KNITTING TAKS OF THE DAY

NOTES

DAILY KNITTING AGENDA

Date:

TO DO:

KNITTING PRIORITIES:

KNITTING QUOTE OF THE DAY:

KNITTING TAKS OF THE DAY

NOTES

DAILY KNITTING AGENDA

Date:

TO DO:

KNITTING PRIORITIES:

KNITTING QUOTE OF THE DAY:

KNITTING TAKS OF THE DAY

NOTES

DAILY KNITTING AGENDA

Date:

TO DO:

-
-
-
-
-
-
-

KNITTING PRIORITIES:

KNITTING QUOTE OF THE DAY:

KNITTING TAKS OF THE DAY

NOTES

DAILY KNITTING AGENDA

Date: _____

TO DO:

KNITTING PRIORITIES:

KNITTING QUOTE OF THE DAY:

KNITTING TAKS OF THE DAY

NOTES

DAILY KNITTING AGENDA

Date:

TO DO:
-
-
-
-
-
-
-

KNITTING PRIORITIES:

KNITTING QUOTE OF THE DAY:

KNITTING TAKS OF THE DAY

NOTES

DAILY KNITTING AGENDA

Date:

TO DO:

KNITTING PRIORITIES:

KNITTING QUOTE OF THE DAY:

KNITTING TAKS OF THE DAY

NOTES

DAILY KNITTING AGENDA

Date:

TO DO:

-
-
-
-
-
-

KNITTING PRIORITIES:

KNITTING QUOTE OF THE DAY:

KNITTING TAKS OF THE DAY

NOTES

DAILY KNITTING AGENDA

Date: _____

TO DO:

KNITTING PRIORITIES:

KNITTING QUOTE OF THE DAY:

KNITTING TAKS OF THE DAY

NOTES

DAILY KNITTING AGENDA

Date:

TO DO:

KNITTING PRIORITIES:

KNITTING QUOTE OF THE DAY:

KNITTING TAKS OF THE DAY

NOTES

DAILY KNITTING AGENDA

Date:

TO DO:

KNITTING PRIORITIES:

KNITTING QUOTE OF THE DAY:

KNITTING TAKS OF THE DAY

NOTES

DAILY KNITTING AGENDA

Date:

TO DO:

KNITTING PRIORITIES:

KNITTING QUOTE OF THE DAY:

KNITTING TAKS OF THE DAY

NOTES

DAILY KNITTING AGENDA

Date:

TO DO:

KNITTING PRIORITIES:

KNITTING QUOTE OF THE DAY:

KNITTING TAKS OF THE DAY

NOTES

DAILY KNITTING AGENDA

Date:

TO DO:

KNITTING PRIORITIES:

KNITTING QUOTE OF THE DAY:

KNITTING TAKS OF THE DAY

NOTES

DAILY KNITTING AGENDA

Date:

TO DO:

KNITTING PRIORITIES:

KNITTING QUOTE OF THE DAY:

KNITTING TAKS OF THE DAY

NOTES

DAILY KNITTING AGENDA

Date:

TO DO:

-
-
-
-
-
-
-
-

KNITTING PRIORITIES:

KNITTING QUOTE OF THE DAY:

KNITTING TAKS OF THE DAY

NOTES

DAILY KNITTING AGENDA

Date:

TO DO:

KNITTING PRIORITIES:

KNITTING QUOTE OF THE DAY:

KNITTING TAKS OF THE DAY

NOTES

DAILY KNITTING AGENDA

Date:

TO DO:

KNITTING PRIORITIES:

KNITTING QUOTE OF THE DAY:

KNITTING TAKS OF THE DAY

NOTES

DAILY KNITTING AGENDA

Date:

TO DO:

KNITTING PRIORITIES:

KNITTING QUOTE OF THE DAY:

KNITTING TAKS OF THE DAY

NOTES

DAILY KNITTING AGENDA

Date: _____

TO DO:
- [ ] _____
- [ ] _____
- [ ] _____
- [ ] _____
- [ ] _____
- [ ] _____

KNITTING PRIORITIES:

KNITTING QUOTE OF THE DAY:

KNITTING TAKS OF THE DAY

NOTES

DAILY KNITTING AGENDA

Date: _____

TO DO:

KNITTING PRIORITIES:

KNITTING QUOTE OF THE DAY:

KNITTING TAKS OF THE DAY

NOTES

DAILY KNITTING AGENDA

Date:

TO DO:

- _____
- _____
- _____
- _____
- _____
- _____
- _____

KNITTING PRIORITIES:

KNITTING QUOTE OF THE DAY:

KNITTING TAKS OF THE DAY

NOTES

DAILY KNITTING AGENDA

Date: _____

TO DO: KNITTING PRIORITIES:

KNITTING QUOTE OF THE DAY:

KNITTING TAKS OF THE DAY

NOTES

DAILY KNITTING AGENDA

Date:

TO DO:

☐ _____
☐ _____
☐ _____
☐ _____
☐ _____
☐ _____
☐ _____
☐ _____

KNITTING PRIORITIES:

KNITTING QUOTE OF THE DAY:

KNITTING TAKS OF THE DAY

NOTES

DAILY KNITTING AGENDA

Date:

TO DO:

KNITTING PRIORITIES:

KNITTING QUOTE OF THE DAY:

KNITTING TAKS OF THE DAY

NOTES

DAILY KNITTING AGENDA

Date:

TO DO:

KNITTING PRIORITIES:

KNITTING QUOTE OF THE DAY:

KNITTING TAKS OF THE DAY

NOTES

DAILY KNITTING AGENDA

Date: _____

TO DO:

KNITTING PRIORITIES:

KNITTING QUOTE OF THE DAY:

KNITTING TAKS OF THE DAY

NOTES

DAILY KNITTING AGENDA

Date:

TO DO:

-
-
-
-
-
-
-

KNITTING PRIORITIES:

KNITTING QUOTE OF THE DAY:

KNITTING TAKS OF THE DAY

NOTES

DAILY KNITTING AGENDA

Date: _____

TO DO:

KNITTING PRIORITIES:

KNITTING QUOTE OF THE DAY:

KNITTING TAKS OF THE DAY

NOTES

DAILY KNITTING AGENDA

Date:

TO DO:

-
-
-
-
-
-
-

KNITTING PRIORITIES:

KNITTING QUOTE OF THE DAY:

KNITTING TAKS OF THE DAY

NOTES

DAILY KNITTING AGENDA

Date: _____

TO DO:

KNITTING PRIORITIES:

KNITTING QUOTE OF THE DAY:

KNITTING TAKS OF THE DAY

NOTES

DAILY KNITTING AGENDA

Date: _____

TO DO:
- ☐ _____
- ☐ _____
- ☐ _____
- ☐ _____
- ☐ _____
- ☐ _____

KNITTING PRIORITIES:

KNITTING QUOTE OF THE DAY:

KNITTING TAKS OF THE DAY

NOTES

DAILY KNITTING AGENDA

Date: _____

TO DO:

KNITTING PRIORITIES:

KNITTING QUOTE OF THE DAY:

KNITTING TAKS OF THE DAY

NOTES

DAILY KNITTING AGENDA

Date:

TO DO:
-
-
-
-
-
-
-

KNITTING PRIORITIES:

KNITTING QUOTE OF THE DAY:

KNITTING TAKS OF THE DAY

NOTES

DAILY KNITTING AGENDA

Date: _____

TO DO:

KNITTING PRIORITIES:

KNITTING QUOTE OF THE DAY:

KNITTING TAKS OF THE DAY

NOTES

DAILY KNITTING AGENDA

Date: _____

TO DO:

- _____
- _____
- _____
- _____
- _____
- _____
- _____
- _____

KNITTING PRIORITIES:

KNITTING QUOTE OF THE DAY:

KNITTING TAKS OF THE DAY

NOTES

DAILY KNITTING AGENDA

Date: _____

TO DO:

KNITTING PRIORITIES:

KNITTING QUOTE OF THE DAY:

KNITTING TAKS OF THE DAY

NOTES

DAILY KNITTING AGENDA

Date:

TO DO:

KNITTING PRIORITIES:

KNITTING QUOTE OF THE DAY:

KNITTING TAKS OF THE DAY

NOTES

DAILY KNITTING AGENDA

Date:

TO DO:

KNITTING PRIORITIES:

KNITTING QUOTE OF THE DAY:

KNITTING TAKS OF THE DAY

NOTES

DAILY KNITTING AGENDA

Date:

TO DO:

-
-
-
-
-
-

KNITTING PRIORITIES:

KNITTING QUOTE OF THE DAY:

KNITTING TAKS OF THE DAY

NOTES

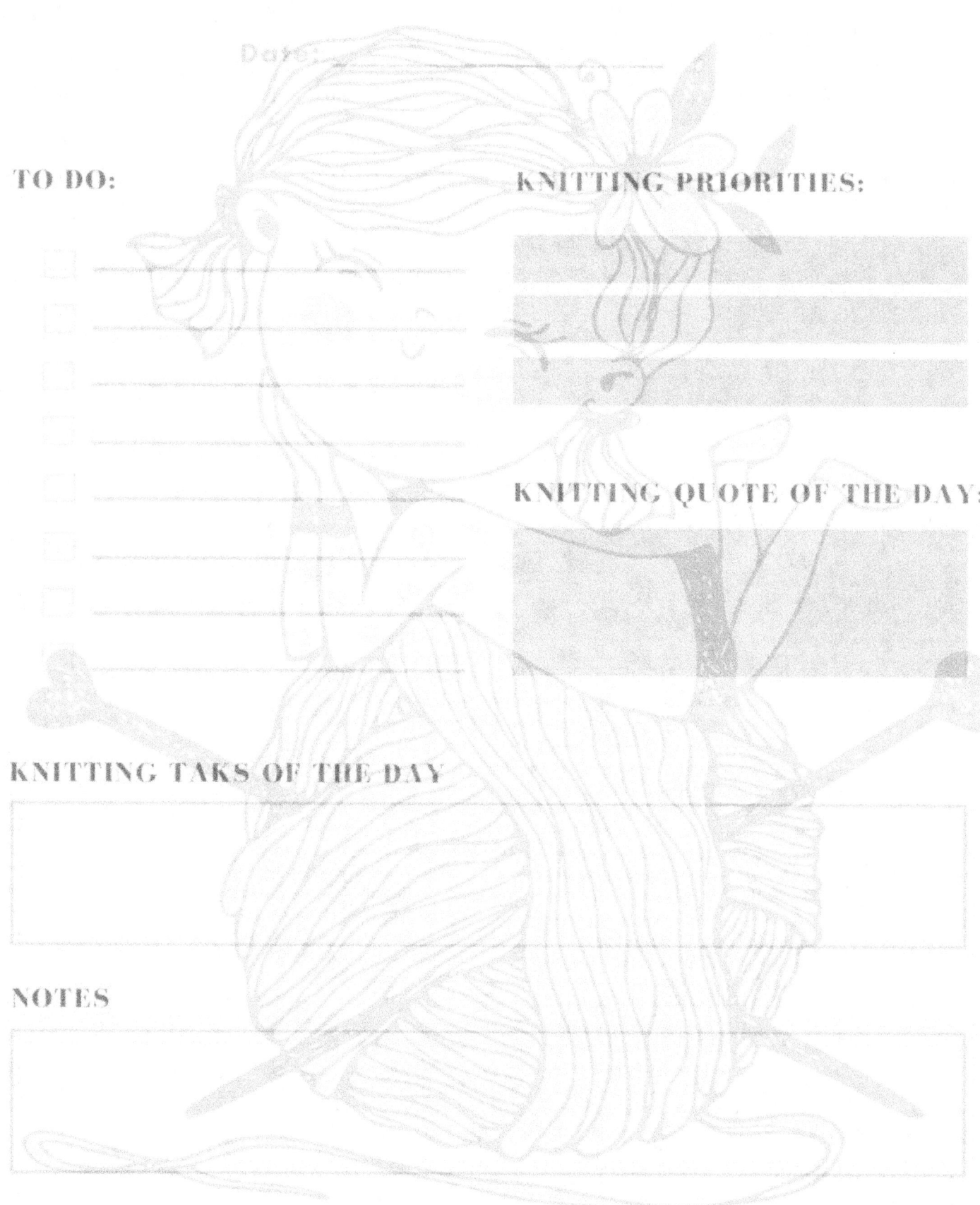

DAILY KNITTING AGENDA

Date:

TO DO:

KNITTING PRIORITIES:

KNITTING QUOTE OF THE DAY:

KNITTING TAKS OF THE DAY

NOTES

DAILY KNITTING AGENDA

Date:

TO DO:

KNITTING PRIORITIES:

KNITTING QUOTE OF THE DAY:

KNITTING TAKS OF THE DAY

NOTES

DAILY KNITTING AGENDA

Date:

TO DO:

KNITTING PRIORITIES:

KNITTING QUOTE OF THE DAY:

KNITTING TAKS OF THE DAY

NOTES

DAILY KNITTING AGENDA

Date:

TO DO:

-
-
-
-
-
-
-

KNITTING PRIORITIES:

KNITTING QUOTE OF THE DAY:

KNITTING TAKS OF THE DAY

NOTES

DAILY KNITTING AGENDA

Date: _____

TO DO:

KNITTING PRIORITIES:

KNITTING QUOTE OF THE DAY:

KNITTING TAKS OF THE DAY

NOTES

DAILY KNITTING AGENDA

Date:

TO DO:

KNITTING PRIORITIES:

KNITTING QUOTE OF THE DAY:

KNITTING TAKS OF THE DAY

NOTES

DAILY KNITTING AGENDA

Date: _____

TO DO:

KNITTING PRIORITIES:

KNITTING QUOTE OF THE DAY:

KNITTING TAKS OF THE DAY

NOTES

DAILY KNITTING AGENDA

Date:

TO DO:

-
-
-
-
-
-

KNITTING PRIORITIES:

KNITTING QUOTE OF THE DAY:

KNITTING TAKS OF THE DAY

NOTES

DAILY KNITTING AGENDA

Date:

TO DO:

KNITTING PRIORITIES:

KNITTING QUOTE OF THE DAY:

KNITTING TAKS OF THE DAY

NOTES

DAILY KNITTING AGENDA

Date:

TO DO:

KNITTING PRIORITIES:

KNITTING QUOTE OF THE DAY:

KNITTING TAKS OF THE DAY

NOTES

DAILY KNITTING AGENDA

Date:

TO DO:

KNITTING PRIORITIES:

KNITTING QUOTE OF THE DAY:

KNITTING TAKS OF THE DAY

NOTES

DAILY KNITTING AGENDA

Date: _____

TO DO:

- _____
- _____
- _____
- _____
- _____
- _____

KNITTING PRIORITIES:

KNITTING QUOTE OF THE DAY:

KNITTING TAKS OF THE DAY

NOTES

DAILY KNITTING AGENDA

Date: _____

TO DO:

KNITTING PRIORITIES:

KNITTING QUOTE OF THE DAY:

KNITTING TAKS OF THE DAY

NOTES

DAILY KNITTING AGENDA

Date:

TO DO:

KNITTING PRIORITIES:

KNITTING QUOTE OF THE DAY:

KNITTING TAKS OF THE DAY

NOTES

DAILY KNITTING AGENDA

Date:

TO DO:

KNITTING PRIORITIES:

KNITTING QUOTE OF THE DAY:

KNITTING TAKS OF THE DAY

NOTES

DAILY KNITTING AGENDA

Date:

TO DO:

-
-
-
-
-
-
-

KNITTING PRIORITIES:

KNITTING QUOTE OF THE DAY:

KNITTING TAKS OF THE DAY

NOTES

DAILY KNITTING AGENDA

Date:

TO DO:

KNITTING PRIORITIES:

KNITTING QUOTE OF THE DAY:

KNITTING TAKS OF THE DAY

NOTES

DAILY KNITTING AGENDA

Date:

TO DO:

KNITTING PRIORITIES:

KNITTING QUOTE OF THE DAY:

KNITTING TAKS OF THE DAY

NOTES

DAILY KNITTING AGENDA

Date:

TO DO:

KNITTING PRIORITIES:

KNITTING QUOTE OF THE DAY:

KNITTING TAKS OF THE DAY

NOTES

DAILY KNITTING AGENDA

Date: _____

TO DO:

☐ _____
☐ _____
☐ _____
☐ _____
☐ _____
☐ _____
☐ _____

KNITTING PRIORITIES:

KNITTING QUOTE OF THE DAY:

KNITTING TAKS OF THE DAY

NOTES

DAILY KNITTING AGENDA

Date: _____

TO DO:

KNITTING PRIORITIES:

KNITTING QUOTE OF THE DAY:

KNITTING TAKS OF THE DAY

NOTES

DAILY KNITTING AGENDA

Date:

TO DO:

KNITTING PRIORITIES:

KNITTING QUOTE OF THE DAY:

KNITTING TAKS OF THE DAY

NOTES

DAILY KNITTING AGENDA

Date:

TO DO:

KNITTING PRIORITIES:

KNITTING QUOTE OF THE DAY:

KNITTING TAKS OF THE DAY

NOTES

DAILY KNITTING AGENDA

Date:

TO DO:

- [ ]
- [ ]
- [ ]
- [ ]
- [ ]
- [ ]
- [ ]

KNITTING PRIORITIES:

KNITTING QUOTE OF THE DAY:

KNITTING TAKS OF THE DAY

NOTES

DAILY KNITTING AGENDA

Date:

TO DO:

KNITTING PRIORITIES:

KNITTING QUOTE OF THE DAY:

KNITTING TAKS OF THE DAY

NOTES

DAILY KNITTING AGENDA

Date:

TO DO:

KNITTING PRIORITIES:

KNITTING QUOTE OF THE DAY:

KNITTING TAKS OF THE DAY

NOTES